JOHN CORIGLIANO

LULLABY FOR NATALIE

FOR VIOLIN AND PIANO

ED 4543
First Printing: February 2015

ISBN: 978-1-4803-6894-1

G. SCHIRMER, *Inc.*

DISTRIBUTED BY

7777 W. BLUEMOUND RD. P.O. BOX 13819 MILWAUKEE, WI 53213

halleonard.com
musicsalesclassical.com

The first performance of "Lullaby for Natalie"
was given on January 30, 2011
by Anne Akiko Meyers, violin
with Reiko Uchida, piano
at the Rubin Museum
New York, NY

Duration 5 minutes

The following is available from the publisher's
Rental and Performance Department
www.musicsalesclassical.com

Lullaby for Natalie (for violin and orchestra)
First Performance July 19, 2014
Eastern Music Festival, Greenville, NC
Jeffrey Multer, violin; Gerard Schwarz, conductor

Lullaby for Natalie (for orchestra)
First Performance August 6, 2011
(under the title Cabrillo Lullaby)
Cabrillo Music Festival, Santa Cruz, CA
Marin Alsop, conductor

The following is available for sale
www.halleonard.com

Lullaby for Natalie (for concert band)
arranged by Peter Stanley Martin
(HL 50499540: score and parts / HL 50499541: score)

for Anne and Natalie

LULLABY FOR NATALIE

John Corigliano

Copyright © 2011 by G. Schirmer Inc. (ASCAP), New York, NY
International Copyright Secured. All Rights Reserved.
Warning: Unauthorized reproduction of this publication is
prohibited by Federal Law and subject to criminal prosecution.

JOHN CORIGLIANO

LULLABY FOR NATALIE

FOR VIOLIN AND PIANO

VIOLIN

ED 4543
First Printing: February 2015

ISBN: 978-1-4803-6894-1

G. SCHIRMER, Inc.

DISTRIBUTED BY

HAL•LEONARD®
CORPORATION
7777 W. BLUEMOUND RD. P.O. BOX 13819 MILWAUKEE, WI 53213

halleonard.com
musicsalesclassical.com

Violin

for Anne and Natalie

LULLABY FOR NATALIE

John Corigliano

Copyright © 2011 by G. Schirmer Inc. (ASCAP), New York, NY
International Copyright Secured. All Rights Reserved.
Warning: Unauthorized reproduction of this publication is
prohibited by Federal Law and subject to criminal prosecution.

* Play with thumb.